UNCLE SANTA
and the
Magic Hot Chocolate

PAGE PUBLISHING, INC.
Conneaut Lake, PA

First originally published by Page Publishing 2021

ISBN 978-1-6624-4591-0 (pbk)
ISBN 978-1-6624-4593-4 (hc)
ISBN 978-1-6624-4592-7 (digital)

Printed in the United States of America

UNCLE SANTA
and the
Magic Hot Chocolate

Book 4
A Birthday Party for Jesus

Lisa Dunn

"Everyone, gather 'round," Uncle Santa said. "I'd like to read you the story about the very first Christmas. The Christmas when baby Jesus was born."

3

All the kids sat around Uncle Santa's chair, laughing and smiling excitedly.

"Once upon a time," Uncle Santa said as he opened the book to page one, "a very long time ago, there was a young girl named Mary."

"An angel told her that she was chosen by God to have a baby boy named Jesus, and he would save the world."

5

"A few months later, Mary and her husband, Joseph, went to Bethlehem. When they got there, they went to the inn to get a room. But there weren't any rooms left. The innkeeper told them that they could stay in the stable. So that is what they did."

"It was time for Mary to have her baby. After Jesus was born, she wrapped him up in blankets and put him in the manger."

"What is a manger?" Josh asked.

"A manger holds hay for the animals to eat, but Mary used the manger for Jesus's crib," Uncle Santa replied.

9

"There were shepherds watching their sheep nearby, and an angel told them, 'A baby has been born, and he is God's Son. You will find the baby wrapped in blankets, sleeping in the manger.' The shepherds went to Bethlehem to see the tiny baby."

There were three wise men who followed the Christmas star that led them to baby Jesus. They brought presents of gold, frankincense, and myrrh.

Uncle Santa closed the book and said, "When Jesus grew up, he traveled all around the world to teach people about the Word of God."

"My Sunday school teacher told us that story when we put the Christmas tree up at church," Olivia said.

"Many people think that a Christmas tree stands for the peace and hope that Jesus brought to the world," said Uncle Santa.

"Our tree has a star on top," Liam said excitedly.

"We put an angel on the top of our tree," Ethan said.

"Both of those are a part of the first Christmas story too," Uncle Santa said. "The angel was the one who told Mary that she was going to have a baby boy, and the Christmas star led the three wise men to Jesus."

"My sister says that when we make a snow angel, it comes back and checks on you at night when you are asleep." Grayson giggled. All the kids laughed.

I BELIEVE IN SANTA CLAUS

15

"We have pretty white lights on our tree," Amanda said, "and red and green ornaments too."

"We have candy canes on our tree," smiled Olivia.

Uncle Santa replied, "Did you know that if you turn the candy cane upside down, it makes the letter *J*, just like the first letter in Jesus's name?"

"Really? I like that," Olivia answered.

17

"My mom put a present for me and my sister under our tree," Caleb said.

"Those presents are like the ones that the three wise men gave to Jesus," Uncle Santa said.

"My mom said that Jesus is the reason for the season," Tommy said.

"That is exactly right," Uncle Santa replied.

Tommy's mother walked into the room to join them at the party. "Uncle Santa read us a story about Jesus," Tommy said to his mother, "and three wise guys brought Jesus presents just like Santa brings presents to me!"

They all laughed, and Tommy thanked Uncle Santa for inviting him to such a fun birthday party.

The kids played games and enjoyed cake and ice cream, singing happy birthday to Jesus.

I BELIEVE IN SANTA CLAUS

23

Uncle Santa asked the kids one final question, "What does Christmas mean to you?"

These are the answers the kids told him:

love
joy
friends
family
giving
having fun
milk and cookies
celebrating
and Jesus

Yes, Jesus is the reason for the season.
Happy birthday, Jesus!

CPSIA information can be obtained
at www.ICGtesting.com
Printed in the USA
LVHW081317250523
748015LV00006B/126